RED WHITE AND BLUE

Susan Canizares • Betsey Chessen

Scholastic Inc.

New York • Toronto • London • Auckland • Sydney

Acknowledgments

Literacy Specialist: Linda Cornwell

Social Studies Consultant: Barbara Schubert, Ph.D.

Design: Silver Editions

Photo Research: Silver Editions

Endnotes: Jacqueline Smith

Endnote Illustrations: Anthony Carnabucia

––––––––––––––––––––

Photographs: Cover: Peter Poulides/Tony Stone Images; p. 1: Inga Spence/The Picture Cube, Inc.; p. 2: Steve Allen/Peter Arnold, Inc.; p. 3: Moggy/Tony Stone Images; p. 4: Patrick W. Grace/Photo Researchers, Inc.; p. 5: Frank Siteman/The Picture Cube, Inc.; p. 6: Kaj R. Svensson/Photo Researchers, Inc.; p. 7: Randy Wells/Tony Stone Images; p. 8: Olney Vasan/Tony Stone Images; p. 9: Doug Armand/Tony Stone Images; pp. 10–11: Werner H. Muller/Peter Arnold, Inc.; p. 12: Peter Poulides/Tony Stone Images.

Library of Congress Cataloging-in-Publication Data
Canizares, Susan, 1960-.
Red, white, and blue / Susan Canizares, Betsey Chessen.
p. cm. -- (Social studies emergent readers)
Summary: Simple text and photographs explore the colors of the American flag and present other American things that are red, white, or blue.
ISBN 0-439-04564-9 (pbk. : alk. paper)
1. Flags--United States--Juvenile literature.
[1. Color. 2. Flags--United States.]
I. Chessen, Betsey, 1970- .
II. Title. III. Series.
CR113.C363 1998

929.920973--dc21

98-47669
CIP AC

14 15 16 17 18 19 20   08   6/0

Red.

White.

Blue.

Red and white.

Blue.

Red and white.

Blue and white.

White, blue,

and red.

Red, white, and blue!

RED WHITE AND BLUE

Red apples Apples are not native to the U.S. They were brought over by the English in the seventeenth century. More than 7,000 types of apples are grown in the U.S., the most common being Red and Golden Delicious, Granny Smith, and Macintosh.

The White House The White House in Washington, D.C., is where the President lives. About 110 people work at the White House, including doctors, cooks, maids, chauffeurs, and Secret Service agents. The President's family lives on the second floor. The President works in a room called the Oval Office.

Blue jeans A tailor named Levi Strauss invented blue jeans in the 1850s. He had come to America to make tents for the gold miners. He didn't sell many tents, so he decided to use the canvas to make pants. He used a cotton fabric imported from the city of Nimes in France. We now call this fabric denim ("de Nimes" means "from Nimes" in French).

Red and white schoolhouse In the last century, schools built in many rural parts of the country were small red and white one-room buildings. In these "little red schoolhouses," children of all different ages and grades were taught in the same room, usually by one teacher. The teacher did not teach all the students at the same time; he or she taught small groups of children in the same grade.

Red and white fire engines Fire trucks were first used in Europe, but the big red hook-and-ladder fire engine that is a familiar sight today was born in San Francisco in 1868. It was an important improvement on the earlier fire engines—the ladders could extend easily and could tilt at any angle.

Blueberries The U.S. and Canada are the biggest producers of blueberries in the world. They often grow wild, but they are also cultivated for the food industry. In the U.S., the biggest producers of blueberries are Maine, Michigan, New Jersey, North Carolina, and Washington.

Blue Ridge Mountains The Blue Ridge Mountains run from Pennsylvania down through Georgia. They got their name because the forests that grow on their slopes look blue from a distance. The mountains are some of the oldest in North America, and have been worn down by wind and water to become smooth in many places.

Baseball A baseball is made of cork and yarn inside, and white cowhide sewn with red thread on the outside. Historians believe that baseball grew out of old English games. The rules and equipment we use today were developed in the mid-1800s. Baseball became so popular all across the country that it is now called "the national pastime."

Blue sky and white clouds When you look up at the sky, clouds look like fluffy pillows, animals, or even faces. Actually, they are just a collection of water droplets. The warmth of the sun makes the water from the earth rise into the sky, where it collects into droplets, which the wind pushes together to make clouds. Cumulus clouds are thick, white, and puffy. When these clouds turn dark, it usually means a thunderstorm is on its way.

White, blue, and red fireworks Fireworks are often part of a Fourth of July celebration. Fireworks were invented by the Chinese centuries ago. A special powder made of charcoal makes them explode when they are lit, and other metal powders give them their colors.

The American flag The United States flag has 13 alternating red and white stripes. These stripes represent the original 13 colonies that formed the United States. The white stars on the blue background represent the 50 states. The flag flies over the White House and the Capitol building in Washington, D.C., every day.